SUMMARY of 13 THINGS MENTALLY STRONG PEOPLE DON'T DO

Take Back Your Power, Embrace Change, Face Your Fears, and Train Your Brain for Happiness and Success

by Amy Morin

A FastReads Book Summary with Key Takeaways & Analysis

Copyright © 2016 by FastReads. All rights reserved. This book or parts thereof may not be reproduced in any form, stored in any retrieval system, or transmitted in any form by any means—electronic, mechanical, photocopy, recording, or otherwise—without prior written permission of the publisher, except as provided by United States of America copyright law. This is an unofficial summary.

TABLE OF CONTENTS

INTRODUCTION
What is Mental Strength?

CHAPTER 1
They Don't Waste Time Feeling Sorry for Themselves

CHAPTER 2
They Don't Give Away Their Power

CHAPTER 3
They Don't Shy Away from Change

CHAPTER 4
They Don't Focus on Things They Can't Control

CHAPTER 5
They Don't Worry About Pleasing Everyone

CHAPTER 6
They Don't Fear Taking Calculated Risks

CHAPTER 7
They Don't Dwell on The Past

CHAPTER 8
They Don't Make the Same Mistakes Over And Over

CHAPTER 9
They Don't Resent Other People's Success

CHAPTER 10
They Don't Give Up After the First Failure

CHAPTER 11
They Don't Fear Alone Time

CHAPTER 12
They Don't Feel the World Owes Them Anything

CHAPTER 13
They Don't Expect Immediate Results

Conclusion on Maintaining Mental Strength

INTRODUCTION

After suddenly losing her mother after a basketball game, her husband dying of a sudden heart attack at age twenty-six, eventually trying new things including motorcycling, remarrying and losing her new father-in-law to cancer, Amy Morin had to be very careful of her mental status.

She knew feeling sorry for herself or feeling overwhelmed would inhibit her from dealing with her pain. As part of the healing, she wrote a list of "13 Things Mentally Strong People Don't Do." These things were bad habits she strived to avoid in order to feel better about herself and her situation. As a therapist, she knew these things, but writing them down helped her focus on what to do to stay strong.

Bad habits have a way of sabotaging mental strength. Good habits are certainly vital, but won't do much good if the bad habits work against them. That struggle creates frustration and prevents goals from being reached. Though good habits may be our priority, not giving attention to the things which undermine the overall goal is self-destructive. Therefore, it is essential to recognize them for what they are.

Key Takeaways:

• The author successfully dealt with tremendous heartache in her adult life.

• She recognized a different approach: avoiding certain behaviors.

• Her goal in the book is to "…help you develop mental strength, which is essential to dealing with life's problems."

What is Mental Strength?

Factors which play a role in how easily you cultivate mental strength are: genetics, personality, and experience. These cannot be changed, but behavior to avoid certain predispositions can be learned. True mental strength demands a three-point attack: Thoughts should be realistic; behaviors must be positive regardless of circumstances; and emotions must be controlled so they don't control you. "Think positive," isn't enough, you need help to reach mental strength.

Mental strength helps you be prepared for unexpected challenges. It increases your resistance to stress, improves your overall satisfaction, and enhances your performance in whatever activity you engage. The checklist is intended to point out the pitfalls of life's challenges, and help you become a better, stronger person.

Key Takeaways:

• Rational thinking and balanced emotions should be used to determine behavior.

• Acting tough is not being mentally strong. Acting according to your values is.

• Don't ignore emotions or treat yourself like a machine. Interpret emotions and do not ignore pain.

• Overthinking positive thoughts can lead to false assumptions.

• Being mentally strong does not bring happiness, but does breed contentedness.

CHAPTER 1
They Don't Waste Time Feeling Sorry for Themselves

Self-pity is self-destructive behavior. It may feel good for a little while, but it will postpone much needed examination of the situation. Self-pity is often used as a way to get attention. The trouble is, attitudes are contagious and other people may brag about their own problems. Feeling grateful for what you have is far better than wallowing in self-pity. The old cliché of "look for the silver lining," will bring much more happiness than thinking negatively.

Ways to avoid falling into self-pity are: keep a gratitude journal every day; tell someone out loud something you are grateful for; shift focus to gratitude when pity sneaks in; and teach others to be grateful. If we are grateful for what we have, we have no room to worry about what we don't have. Never exaggerate the questionable situation. Always be proactive in problem-solving and thinking positively.

Key Takeaways:

• Humans are more skilled at offering good advice to others, and forgetting to take that same advice in their own lives.

• Self-pity is rooted in a lack of confidence. Think of successes which will build your confidence and pull you out of pity.

• Make a list of good things in your life. Then when bad stuff happens, refer to that list.

• Notice the good in the world. Recognize how others are kind and generous and you will have greater appreciation for your situation.

• Gratitude leads to happiness, improves the ability to forgive, makes you more accepting and outgoing, and you won't get sick as often.

CHAPTER 2
They Don't Give Away Their Power

To avoid giving away power, healthy boundaries must be in place. Setting limits on what you will tolerate from others will relieve stress. Boundaries are not disrespectful. Many problems arise from the lack of boundaries: your feelings rely on others; you avoid the real issue; you believe you are a victim; you are very sensitive to criticism; you are not focused on your own goals; you may feel resentment for people who "step on your toes."

Adjust how you look at a situation. Avoid phrases like: He MADE me mad; I'm just not good enough; I HAVE to go. Only you control your emotions and choices. You may need to excuse or distract yourself from the problem for a while to take deep breaths and cultivate rational thoughts. When receiving criticism, stop and evaluate if there is evidence to support or refute the statement and examine why the person is telling you this. Only then decide if you need to change your behavior.

Key Takeaways:

• Not setting heathy boundaries risks giving your power away.

• If other people are allowed to define your self-worth, you'll never feel truly worthy.

• Putting up healthy boundaries may cause some trouble, but you will learn to live with it.

• If you don't wish people to be a major force in your life, stop giving them your time and effort.

• Always be aware the opinion of one person does not equate to fact. You can rise above that opinion and cease giving any time or energy to hopeless disagreement.

• Remind yourself there are choices in everything you do. This can make you feel free.

CHAPTER 3
They Don't Shy Away from Change

There are many ways to avoid change, most do not support mental strength—such as justifying a bad habit by saying is isn't all that bad. Or maybe you get anxious or are wishy-washy about handling change. Worse, when in a bad situation, change can be resisted because that change might be for the worse. You make excuses for avoiding change. Granted, uncomfortable sensations may appear with change, but the mind must be prepared to take on the challenge, not wimp out and stay in the same place. You have to be ready for the change and commit to it in order to be successful. Maintenance of the support for change is often forgotten. Plan to incorporate it into every part of your life.

Changing for change's sake isn't enough, however. You must understand the reasons for the change to determine what is best. Make goals regarding the change, be accountable to yourself or someone else, and make allowances for obstacles which might occur. Yes, change can be uncomfortable, but unless you are willing to grow and move forward with your life, you won't be able to increase mental strength. Positive change leads to improved motivation, and improved motivation leads to even more positive change. It's good for you in both directions.

Key Takeaways:

• Beware of changing too much too fast. It is a recipe for disaster.

• Do not give up on the change just because it is difficult. Follow through.

• You may have to build confidence in tolerating discomfort prior to implementing change.

• Grief—an intense emotion—hinders change by our attempts to avoid it.

• First change yourself, and then your life will make a difference for others.

• Manage negative thoughts and watch for those who influence your decision making.

• If the change involves personality, behave like the person you want to be.

CHAPTER 4
They Don't Focus on Things They Can't Control

In an effort to control one's own anxiety, one may try to control everything. Or you may suffer from a "superhero complex" where you feel you must fix everything and can if you try hard enough. You want it "done right" so believe you have to do it yourself. But this leads to anxiety. Being concerned about things out of your control wastes your time and energy. It damages relationships and undermines trust. And you may blame yourself for everything that is wrong in the world.

You must focus on only those things you can control. For example: you can hold a great party, but you cannot make people have fun. Or, having the best possible attitude will not cure a disease. When dealing with loved ones, it is difficult to sit by and allow them to make mistakes. Instead of fussing or nagging, however, you should listen carefully, share your opinion only once, and find something positive to discuss. Remember, only you have control over you. When you stop trying to control everything else, you'll feel happier, less stressed, have better relationships, and enjoy success.

Key Takeaways:

• Don't waste your time and energy preparing for something bad to happen, concentrate instead on preparing for something good to happen.

• Focusing on controlling everything only takes away from what you can actually control.

• When trying to control something you cannot, ask, *what am I so afraid of?* That someone will make a bad choice? That something will go terribly wrong? Recognizing those fears and learning to handle them will give you the mental strength to focus on only what you can control.

• Blaming yourself for bad things happening out of your control is destructive. You are not responsible for things over which you have no control.

CHAPTER 5
They Don't Worry About Pleasing Everyone

Having self-worth determined by how other people see you is a hole into which you may fall. We fear conflict and often avoid it by trying to make everyone happy. It is somewhat of a learned behavior to try not to displease others to avoid some other bad situation. But in the process, you lose your own self value. It may seem like being generous and idealistic, but a people-pleaser is really a selfish person—they think everyone should care about what they do.

Time should be taken when faced with a situation to consider whether you will say yes or no. Determine if you want the situation to happen, what you will have to sacrifice to make it happen, what you will gain, and how you will feel afterward. This will require you to be assertive and stay true to yourself.

Key Takeaways:

• Excessive people-pleasing is actually an attempt at controlling how others feel.

• Trying to please everyone is a waste of your time and energy because you can't control them anyway.

• Manipulative people will take advantage of people-pleasers.

• Do not change your values or behavior when someone is angry or emotionally distraught. It is not your responsibility to make them happy.

• Do not be afraid to say no.

CHAPTER 6
They Don't Fear Taking Calculated Risks

Fear of the unknown is basically what drives the fear of taking risks. Whether it be in business, a dream, or you believe you have bad luck, fear of taking risks hinders productive action. Calculating the risk is vital. If you can project the possibility of your actions manifesting in either positive or negative results, then you can calculate the impact of those results. Avoid using emotions or falling back on habits. If you're feeling down, that sadness may affect your decision. Conversely, feeling happy and optimistic may cause you to overlook a valid risk. Venturing into the unknown and taking a well-thought out, calculated risk can help you find success and mental strength.

Calculate your risk by asking the following questions:

What are the potential costs? Benefits?

How will this affect my goals?

What are the alternatives?

What is the best thing and the worst thing that can happen?

How much will this matter in five years?

Write down the answers to these questions and review. Examine the decision carefully.

Key Takeaways

• Do not shy away from risk. Instead examine and calculate it in order to make a decision.

• Think about "what could be," not, "what if."

• Beware of not separating what is influencing your emotions. One obscure fear can affect an unrelated decision.

• Recognize the difference between skill and chance. Throwing the dice harder will not affect the outcome.

• Practice taking risks and facing fears. If you are afraid to speak in public, do it. If you fear flying, fly. Be open to opportunities and face your fears.

CHAPTER 7
They Don't Dwell on The Past

Dwelling on the past prevents you from focusing on the present and being the best you can be. There may exist a fear of moving on from the past which allows guilt and negative emotions to fester. What has happened in the past cannot be changed or altered and the emotions related to those memories may affect your ability to make healthy decisions in the present.

Thinking of the past affects your current emotional state, so schedule a designated time to think about it. Move your thoughts to something in the present. Keep in mind, memories are often much better or worse than the actual occurrence. When dealing with negative memories, recall the lesson you learned from that experience—focus on the facts, not the emotions, and look at the situation objectively.

Key Takeaways:

• If you think about the past all the time, there is no room for new and positive memories to occur.

• Romanticizing the past is much like believing the grass is greener on the other side. You may be exaggerating how great things used to be.

• Give yourself permission to live in the now. You are not abandoning the memories, but you must live your present life.

• Forgive. Forgiving past actions by others, or even of yourself, relieves you of the burden of carrying that emotion.

• Staying mired in the past keeps you from appreciating the present.

CHAPTER 8
They Don't Make the Same Mistakes Over And Over

Making mistakes can become habitual. Constantly believing people are against you, or even planning too far ahead for an event. Add in the truth that it is difficult to stray from what we learned as children or in younger years and the same mistakes can become routine. Denying making a mistake makes you more likely to repeat it. Strangely, a person may feel comfortable in this cycle, as they cannot see any other option. But making the same mistakes over and over only leads to problems. Goals cannot be achieved. Problems will not be solved. Your actions may frustrate others. Irrational beliefs may be invented to justify the mistakes.

To avoid making the same mistake, study it. Step out of the negative emotions and look objectively at what caused the mistake. Find an explanation—not an excuse. Ask: what went wrong? What could I have done better? What can I do differently? Find the right path to lead you past the mistake. Replace any behavior which led to the mistake. Watch for that wrong path and avoid it. Make yourself accountable—do not hide the mistake. Always "own up" to your mistake, accepting the responsibility. This will put you in control of yourself and lead to mental strength.

Key Takeaways:

• Avoid being stubborn about the mistake. This leads to repeating the problem

• You can enhance your self-control by practicing tolerating discomfort, using realistic affirmations, focusing on goals, imposing restrictions on your behavior, and creating a comprehensive list of why you should not repeat the mistake. Keep that list with you to refer to when tempted into old patterns.

• Learning from your mistakes will help you grow stronger mentally.

• You should strive to not make excuses and to not be impulsive. Do not set yourself up for failure by getting in situations which hinder rational thought.

CHAPTER 9
They Don't Resent Other People's Success

Resentment is far beyond envy. When you think you want what they have and for them not to have it, you have ventured into an unhealthy behavior. If you are happy when a successful person has troubles or feel negatively toward people who achieve their dreams, you can behave in an illogical way and stray from your own course to success. Insecurity is the root of these types of feelings. If you feel badly about yourself, you'll have a hard time being happy about someone else's accomplishments. You may not even know what it is that you truly want. This resentment can eat up your time and even your life, as you'll be distracted from your own path, will never be content, you will belittle your own skills, and even damage your relationships.

You must look objectively at the situation to more accurately determine reasonable expectations. Don't cloud the issue with past experiences which do not support you. If you do not feel good about yourself, examine why. Find a different way to approach things to temper your attitude toward other's prosperity. Healthy relationships cannot be maintained in a competitive atmosphere. Find ways to build people up, not ways to grind them into the ground. When you can be happy when other people have success, you will in turn attract success to you. Only then can you create your own definition of success, instead of striving toward someone else's.

Key Takeaways:

• Do not compare yourself to other people. Do not focus on things you do not have. Stop saying life isn't fair. Do not diminish others' accomplishments.

• Live according to your own definition of success, not someone else's.

• Document your definition of success. If you are tempted to resent someone's accomplishment, refer to your list to adhere to your own path. Your journey is unique and you will feel relieved and happy that you are not in competition with anyone else.

• Learn to celebrate other people's accomplishments. It makes them and you feel good.

CHAPTER 10
They Don't Give Up After the First Failure

Often people believe if they failed once, they will fail again. It is likely the fear of that that causes them to avoid the possibility of another failure. They give up instead of facing those fears. Giving up can also be learned in childhood. Parents who help their children too much fail to encourage independent thinking. But being afraid of failure hinders you from learning from mistakes, and means you are less likely to move forward.

Studies show extensive practice at a certain skill is more effective than natural talent. Emotional fortitude leads to success more than a high IQ. Blaming a failure on a lack of ability leads to a feeling of helplessness and inability to try again after a failure. Try to understand that failure is not as bad as you may think. Thomas Edison had thousands of failures and learned thousands of ways not to do something.

Key Takeaways:

• Convince yourself of these facts: Failure is part of becoming a success. You can handle and learn from failure. A sign you are being challenged is to accept failure and try again. You can choose to overcome failure.

• Don't allow inaccurate beliefs about your abilities keep you from achieving success.

• If you, as a leader, determine others are only saying what you want to hear and not offering true information, look at yourself. Ask a peer, not an employee. Or if the employees are treating you as another manager wished to be treated, talk about the problem in a group meeting and advise that all your ideas can be questioned.

• Prepare to fail a lot. If you get used to it, it isn't as frightening.

• Decide if the failure is truly important in your grand scheme. If not, you can choose not to try again with validity.

• Create a plan to learn from your failures to avoid repeating them. This is character building and challenging.

CHAPTER 11
They Don't Fear Alone Time

Today's society has a phobia about being alone. If you are uncomfortable with silence, think you must always be doing something, or equate being alone with being lonely, you are missing a powerful opportunity. Research has shown spending time alone in nature results in renewal and rest. Don't try to drown your thought with technology or sounds. Designate ten minutes each day to do nothing but attend to your emotions, body, and goals in life. This can be in meditation or writing in a journal. Turn off the radio in the car or the television when you aren't watching. Go on a quiet walk without your phone. These actions can decrease anxiety and even depression.

Mindfulness raises awareness causing you to accept yourself in the moment. This is useful in alone time and makes it more valuable. Learning meditation and mindfulness can increase your quality of life and help you be comfortable with solitude.

Key Takeaways:

• You must take time to reflect within yourself to become mentally strong.

• Solitude is choosing to be along with your thoughts.

• Practice mindfulness by being very aware of the moment. Savor the bite of food, focus on a few breaths, feel every sensation. Much research tells us mindfulness can be the key to happiness.

• Learn to love silence, taking a few minutes every day to experience it. Schedule the time.

• Discover the benefits of meditation.

CHAPTER 12
They Don't Feel the World Owes Them Anything

To think you are the center of attention and believe you are owed something is neither true nor healthy. It is a way of acting superior to other people and not accepting personal responsibility. You will not earn respect based on merit if you have an entitlement mentality. You will not be able to have a meaningful relationship for being too focused on yourself. A lack of self-awareness is evident in people who act entitled.

Focus on giving, not taking. Be a team player and pay attention to your effort, not your self-perceived importance. You must take time to reflect within yourself to become mentally strong.

Key Takeaways:

- Develop your own sense of self-esteem.

- Don't keep score of your good deeds or the ways you've been wronged.

- Stop and think what other people feel—develop empathy.

CHAPTER 13
They Don't Expect Immediate Results

If you scoff at the old saying "good things come to those who wait," or you want things done right now, or if patience is not one of your virtues, you are on a path to disappointment. A quick solution is not what mentally strong people want. They keep the goal in mind and take whatever steps are needed to reach it. They celebrate milestones to show progress. They resist immediate gratification in favor of a more valuable result.

Key Takeaways:

• Though we live in a face-paced world, everything can't happen instantly.

• Solitude is choosing to be along with your thoughts.

• Establish reasonable expectations—do not grab at a quick fix.

• Delaying gratification leads to lower anxiety.

CONCLUSION
On Maintaining Mental Strength

Mental strength will require maintenance just as physical strength. And it can always be improved. The problems, bad days, extreme emotions, and unproductive behavior will sometimes occur, but the mental strength will guide you through and lessen them in the long haul. Try to improve each day by monitoring your behavior, regulating your emotions, and thinking about your thoughts. Ask for help when you need it from supportive people.

Key Takeaways:

• Remember you don't have to be the best at everything, just the best you can be.

• By becoming mentally strong, you will achieve your best self, have courage to do what is right, and be comfortable with yourself and your capabilities.

END

If you enjoyed this summary, please an honest review on Amazon.com!

Here are some other available titles from FastReads we think you'll enjoy:

Summary of Ego is the Enemy: by Ryan Holiday

Summary of Tribe: by Sebastian Junger

Summary of You Are a Badass: by Jen Sincero

Summary of Grit: by Angela Duckworth

A *FAST READS* PUBLICATION

Made in the USA
San Bernardino, CA
24 December 2016